602
REASONS TO BE
TICKED OFF

602
REASONS TO BE
TICKED OFF

by Comedian
PAUL NARDIZZI

**Andrews McMeel
Publishing**

Kansas City

04 05 06 07 08 BID 10 9 8 7 6 5 4 3 2 1

Library of Congress Catalog Control Number: 2004109154

ISBN: 0-7407-4761-4

Book design by Holly Camerlinck
Book composition by Steve Brooker

Attention: Schools and Businesses
Andrews McMeel books are available at quantity discounts with bulk purchase for educational, business, or sales promotional use. For information, please write to: Special Sales Department, Andrews McMeel Publishing, 4520 Main Street, Kansas City, Missouri 64111.

This book is dedicated to nobody.

Forced to choose, I'd probably go with myself,
organic farmers, and my sister Lynne, whose laugh
I hear in the back of the club even when she's not there.

CONTENTS

vii

ACKNOWLEDGMENTS

I would like to thank myself for all the work I did on this book. I enjoyed the pleasure of my company and hope to collaborate again in the future. I also want to thank God, my family, Stephanie Bennett for getting this project going, Andrews McMeel, and of course all the dumb, miserable maggots on the planet who inspired this book.

EVERYDAY LIFE

602 REASONS TO BE TICKED OFF

Trying to get a check into a parking
ticket envelope and needing a
shoehorn to complete the task.

■

The annoying hissing noise Canadian Geese
make when you chase their babies around
the park with a sledge hammer.

■

Shaking hands with some brainless
clamhead who squeezes so hard
he goes around thinking your
name is Letgo.

Receiving your bill from a hotel and there's a fifty-cent charge for the call you made down to the lobby to ask how much a phone call costs.

602 REASONS TO BE TICKED OFF

When your pinheaded child fiddles with the TV remote over the course of a weekend and accidentally orders two hundred dollars worth of porn, none of which you even get to watch.

■

Hotels that claim they won't put the movie title you rented on the bill, as if it's not blatantly obvious you rented a skin flick when a regular movie costs ten dollars and the one you watched cost forty-seven and has an hour remaining.

When pay-per-view seduces you with a sexy title like *Lick Me,* which turns out to be a documentary on stamps.

WHAT TO DO:

Seduce the cable company by sending them a check with a number in the amount section that is not even close to the paltry sum you have in the bank.

Looking up a word in the dictionary and having no clue what any of the words in the definition mean, either.

Picking up a person for a date who looks ten times worse than the person you met at the bar after you threw up.

■

Going to a zoo where every animal is either underneath a boulder or lying out in the open totally blitzed on tranquilizer juice.

■

Taking your kids to the zoo and all the animals are right up next to the glass having intercourse with one another.

602 REASONS TO BE TICKED OFF

Making out with someone who has a massive overbite and ending up with three chipped teeth and a fat lip.

■

Trying to romantically kiss your lover and they burp in your mouth.

■

When the scan button on your radio gets jammed, causing you to listen to ten million very short songs going down the highway.

Popping a champagne cork and half the booze ends up in the rug.

■

Your spouse catching you sucking alcohol out of the carpet.

■

Weather scientists insisting that there will be another ice age in a billion years, yet the next day's forecast is still up in the air.

602 REASONS TO BE TICKED OFF

Squeezing the front brakes of a bike and going headfirst over the handlebars, and because your feet are strapped to the pedals, the bike stays adhered to your ass and pile drives your skull to the pavement.

■

Debating evolution with a jaw-jutted, head-scratching moron who insists man didn't descend from apes.

■

Stuttering idiots who correct *your* English.

When you tell some ignoramus what city you live in, and they say, "Oh, do you know my friend Henry?"

■

Smokers blowing their foul carcinogens in your face, figuring if they're going to damage their own bodies, they may as well bring along a few hostages.

■

War veterans who pull you aside to show you an actual German head, a bullet hole in their ass, and their one remaining nut.

---

602 REASONS TO BE TICKED OFF

Spending the bulk of the evening trying to pick up a woman in a bar, then suddenly realizing "she" has the voice of a man and her Adam's apple is the size of a meatball at Denny's.

■

An imbecilic golfer yelling "Fore," two minutes after you've been read your last rites and had your eyeball donated to science.

■

Missing eight songs at a rock concert because you're in the men's room waiting behind a drug addict who can't locate his genitals.

Some soup-brained cluckhead turning the lights on in the middle of the night because he "Just wanted to see if you were awake."

602 REASONS TO BE TICKED OFF

Cheap bastards offering you gas money only if you happen to go to the gas station along the way, as if the gas that was already in your tank when you picked them up was paid for by OPEC.

■

Hitting the punch line of a solid joke and nobody getting it, so you keep adding on to the story, and five minutes later you're still filibustering with an ending nowhere in sight.

WHAT TO DO:

End it with something bizarre. If you are telling a joke about two Polish guys on a train, for example, introduce a third person out of nowhere and say, "And then the hairy Russian broad cut off her foot, moved to India, and got impregnated by the Dalai Lama." Then slap your knee and say, "I knew you guys wouldn't get it. Too political for you clowns." Guaranteed at least two of them say, "Oh, now I get it. That's a good one!"

602 REASONS TO BE TICKED OFF

Telling a joke to a moron who laughs all the way through the setup, then you hit the punch line and he says, "That was a lousy joke."

■

Catching the garter at a wedding and having to roll it up the hairy, cellulite-ridden calf of some despondent woman who broke the best man's coccyx diving for the bouquet.

Friends whose house has an odor you can't
stand, so you invite them to your house
and realize *they're* the ones who smell like
a pile of donkey manure.

■

**Some feebleminded relative taking an
ugly picture of you, blowing it up to
poster size, and displaying it in the
entranceway of their house.**

■

As a dog is humping your leg, the
owner just looks at the beast and says,
"How about that?"

602 REASONS TO BE TICKED OFF

Hypocritical dog owners not caring if
their dog humps your leg, but getting
all annoyed by you turning the tables
and humping their dog.

■

 # WHAT TO DO: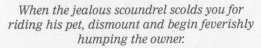

*When the jealous scoundrel scolds you for
riding his pet, dismount and begin feverishly
humping the owner.*

Spending a thousand dollars getting your dog spayed, then finding out that she was already impregnated by a wolf.

■

Inconsiderate louses leaving a centiliter of milk in the fridge, just in case anybody wanted to give their corn flake a sponge bath.

■

Buffoons screaming, "Who had gas?" when it's obvious it was them because the odor hasn't even departed their area yet.

Halitosis-ridden pinheads mangling a tube of toothpaste so that when you squeeze it, the brush remains dry but you're left holding five ounces of gunk.

Making an appointment to see the
doctor and having to tell the chuckling
answering-service operator about
your rectal problems.

■

High-pitched, no-talent dingbats going
around crooning annoying jingles you can't
get out of your head until you park your
skull next to a radio for twenty minutes.

602 REASONS TO BE TICKED OFF

When you're swimming in a public pool and some backstroking moron who can't even see where he's going belts you in the face, and as he swims over you, delivers a dozen flutter kicks to the side of your head.

■

WHAT TO DO:

Stand on the diving board and when the shower-capped idiot comes down into the deep end, land a cannonball right on his chest. If he resurfaces, swim across his body doing the butterfly. Make sure to shove his head under with a two-hand butterfly thrust and then land him a double mule kick to his oxygen-deprived cranium.

Your piss coming out in three separate streams, none of which is headed anywhere near a toilet.

■

Stupid mulyaks using their fingers to put quotes around what they're saying, as if you can't figure out who the hell's talking.

■

Running full tilt into a closed sliding glass door, and having some idiot say, "Did you think that was open?"

602 REASONS TO BE TICKED OFF

Some oaf with no money, job, or education pulling you aside and saying, "Okay, here's what I would do if I was in your situation."

■

Thickheaded pedestrians wearing headphones with no idea that you're blasting your horn and are two feet away from crushing their skeletons.

■

Thoroughly enjoying yourself whaling on some moron, then looking down and realizing you killed the bastard.

Some filthy sloth borrowing your deodorant and depositing a nest of armpit hairs on the surface.

602 REASONS TO BE TICKED OFF

Dumbasses giving you a lousy gift and saying, "I kept the receipt in case you want to return that," so instead of a gift you end up with a pain-in-the-ass errand.

■

Your father telling you a firm handshake will carry you far in the world and then introducing you to a billionaire missing both hands and a trillionaire whose hand feels like a sack of snorts.

■

Spending ten minutes trying to find the handle to shut a sliding glass door, then realizing it's already closed.

Clearing out an entire area so a tree you're chopping down can fall safely, then watching it fall the other way onto your house.

■

Inconsiderate scumbags putting so much bubble gum on the underside of a chair that there is no room for your piece.

■

Speeding through a major city, unable to lose the three squeegee-toting bums clinging for dear life to your windshield wipers.

602 REASONS TO BE TICKED OFF

Pretending to enjoy making out with a woman who has sideburns and a beard.

■

Taking a pill for heartburn that gives you diarrhea, which means all you've done is shifted the burning sensation down to your ass.

■

Watching your children grow up into assholes.

Tracing all your health problems back to the day you asininely used a Porta-Potti.

■

A bunch of punks thrusting a Porta-Potti down the side of a mountain while you're in there naked.

■

Trying to convince the cleaners to accept the clothes you were wearing when you were trapped in a capsized Porta-Potti.

602 REASONS TO BE TICKED OFF

The pathetic control inside the Porta-Potti allowing you to tell those outside that the booth is "Not vacant," as if people who are stupid enough to use the rancid apparatus have anything above a second-grade vocabulary.

■

The unreliable latching system and lack of a men's/women's room sign on the Porta-Potti causing everyone and their mother to walk in on you while your ass is hovering over the Purple Lagoon.

The utter dipshits who are coordinating an event placing one Porta-Potti on the grounds for a massive crowd attending a Baked Bean Festival.

■

Frigging boneheads taking slow, leisurely dumps and browsing the *Times* while there are a thousand people waiting in line for the Porta-Potti.

602 REASONS TO BE TICKED OFF

Porta-Potti manufacturers that color these mobile cesspools blue and green when they should all be dark brown with skulls and crossbones plastered all over the sides and huge DO NOT ENTER signs nailed to the boarded-up doors.

■

Pea-brained security guards not seeming to fathom why on earth you just emptied your bowels right next to the Porta-Potti, instead of risking your life by going *in it*.

JOBS

Getting turned down by some incredibly loose coworker who has slept with everyone in the company except you and the janitor.

Your boss constantly saying, "Look busy," which totally backs up what you've been saying on your memos since you started working there— there's absolutely zilch to do.

Secretaries demanding you call them administrative assistants, as if that's going to change the fact that all you need this gofer for is to get you coffee and a Danish, and file a whole bunch of shit immediately.

602 REASONS TO BE TICKED OFF

Scumbag job interviewers interrupting you when you are discussing your faults to say, "We'll be in touch."

■

Being interviewed by some disheveled bonehead who has the audacity to ask you what *your* job qualifications are.

■

Dishonest sack-of-crap job interviewers saying "We'll get back to you," as if anyone ever gets back to you after chucking your résumé in the trash and calling you a liar.

Falling asleep during a second job interview right after telling the clown that you're a hard worker with loads of energy.

Finicky bosses getting their boxer shorts in a bind just because you call in sick your first ten days on the job, then on the eleventh you take a personal day to sort out a few odds and ends.

602 REASONS TO BE TICKED OFF

Job interviewers wanting to know all about your last job, as if it's some kind of fairy tale that brought you in front of this nitwit's desk begging for a job stacking boxes of underwear.

■

Having to get up and walk out of a job interview because the nosy bastard starts peeking into your criminal record.

Walking out of an interview and realizing your fly was open, your shoes were on the wrong feet, and you had a twenty-foot-long piece of toilet paper tucked into your undies.

602 REASONS TO BE TICKED OFF

Getting a "promotion" and then finding out that the clown you replaced is now doing your job and was told by the same conniving scum that *he* was getting promoted.

■

Staggering into a job interview and realizing the interviewer is the same man who saw you in the parking lot at 7 a.m. smoking joints, sucking down a six-pack, and pleasuring yourself over a copy of *Hustler*.

Anal human resource people getting their underwear all in knots just because you interviewed at IBM but never actually *ran* the joint like you claimed.

■

Describing your weaknesses to a job interviewer and then realizing you probably should have stopped twenty minutes ago when his mouth dropped wide open.

602 REASONS TO BE TICKED OFF

A job interviewer asking if you lie, make a lot of mistakes, or use foul language, and you inadvertently blurt out, "Nope, oops, aw shit!"

■

Spending one hundred grand on a college education, then finding yourself working in a rotting warehouse for a guy named Mongo.

■

Calling in sick to a boss who has caller ID and having to explain to the educationally deprived moron that lap dances help cure sore throats.

Working your tail off for thirty years and all you have to show for it is runny bowel movements, a dilapidated house, and three unemployed kids drinking and partying off your meager wages.

Cheap-assed companies that give you a company car that breaks down more than the crumpled heap of shit you were previously driving.

Telling someone what your salary and occupation are, and them answering, "No really, what do you do?"

■

Strike settlements that put an end to loafing around the house in a drunken stupor.

■

Your shoddy company rewarding you for fifty years of service by offering you a free lunch down in the scumhole cafeteria.

Having to do the work for the entire department because the women are working their tails off nuzzling the boss's new baby, and the rest of the cretins are all in the copy room staring dumbfounded at a carton of toner.

■

Bringing important mail down to the lamebrains in the mailroom and catching the fruitless numbskulls playing Wiffle ball with a rolled-up wad of confidential documents.

602 REASONS TO BE TICKED OFF

Pretentious pain-in-the-scrotum security guards insisting you pop open your trunk and spread 'em for a daily cavity search, despite the fact that these minimum wage crudbags have seen you every day for the last forty-six years.

■

Whaling on the front-gate security guard, then realizing the "unprovoked" attack was caught on tape by sixteen different cameras.

Your company sending recently hired people to Hawaii for training, so you get the pleasure of working alongside a pack of unprepared, extremely dark idiots.

602 REASONS TO BE TICKED OFF

Trying to train an addled pinhead who, instead of looking at the computer screen, stares directly at your face the whole time and says, "I don't know what the heck you are talking about."

■

When some worthless nippleskull costs the company millions with another one of his screw-ups, and you get blamed because you trained the reefer-inhaling skink.

■

Being unable to tune out nearby coworkers whispering your name and the words "Complete jackass."

Glancing at the clock thinking
eight hours have gone by but it's only
been six seconds.

■

Offering up a new idea at a meeting and
your mullet-headed boss says, "Please, that's
ridiculous!" then launches into a plan that's
exactly the same as what you just said, and
all the ass kissers start patting him on the
back and telling him what a genius he is as
opposed to that other nimrod who spoke out.

602 REASONS TO BE TICKED OFF

Your scurrilous manager earning ten times what you do for hiring nitwits like yourself, walking around saying, "Look busy," and embarking on three-hour pilgrimages to the men's room.

■

Getting hired by some disastrous organization whose training program consists of a cabal of waffleheads shouting over the walls of their cubicle, "Figure it out yourself. I'm busy, you dumb oaf!"

Having to learn how to nap with your
eyes open because your desk is
located near the boss's.

 **WHAT TO DO:**

Wear sunglasses at your desk. Tell your boss,
"When I really focus on what I am doing, I get
in a zone and sometimes make snoring noises,
drool, and yell out the names of my former
lovers. Don't interrupt me or you'll throw my
production off big time."

Your skinflinted boss giving you the six-figure salary you asked for—four figures before the decimal and two after it.

The ignoramus behind the security
desk refusing to let you enter
the building without showing your
badge, despite the fact that he
carpooled in with you.

 WHAT TO DO:

*Drive your car up to or, if possible, into the
lobby and yell out the window, "Does this look
familiar, you badge-inspecting dolt?" When
you pick him up the next morning, don't allow
the uniformed pinhead into the car unless he
shows ten forms of identification and supplies
you with a copy of his dental records.*

602 REASONS TO BE TICKED OFF

Your overbearing boss giving you three huge projects and you haven't even taken the paper clips off the two he gave you seventeen years ago.

■

Finally finishing one of your boss's assignments and proudly bringing it to him, only to find he doesn't work there anymore.

■

Company elevators that drop sixty floors in five seconds and constantly have fresh puke coating the walls.

Adding a long column of numbers six different times and getting six different totals.

■

 # WHAT TO DO:

Go with the first one. If the boss comes out and says, "These figures aren't even close," hand him the other five and say, "I got a good hunch it's one of those. Number three really strikes my fancy. If those don't work out, there's plenty more where they came from. I got numbers coming out of my ass over here."

602 REASONS TO BE TICKED OFF

Going through the job listings and seeing your old job listed at twice the salary you were making.

■

Discovering the person you flipped off on the highway is your new boss.

■

People who accomplish nothing all day except leaning back in their chairs, surveying the entire department, and remarking, "We got a bunch of idiots working here."

Your moronic secretary ineffectively covering the mouthpiece of the phone, so the higher-up on the other end hears you say, "What does that old bastard want now?"

The fact that we have a holiday for secretaries so the really important people who make the company run go totally unnoticed while some brainless wonder who flunked out of fifth grade is showered with gifts for saying, "Hello," and then transferring calls to the outside world.

602 REASONS TO BE TICKED OFF

After telling your mind-numbingly dumb assistant to "Hold my calls!!" the halfwit transfers about nine in to you over the next five minutes, then proceeds to tell visitors to "Go right in. He's expecting you."

■

Anal companies failing to recognize the humor when you come back from lunch totally bombed and have no idea where you left your trousers.

Companies putting visitor parking spots right up next to the building, but making the people who actually work there hoof it nine miles across a barren wasteland while some drugged-up lunatic does doughnuts around them in the company security van.

■

Bosses constantly letting you know that they are the boss, as if you need to be reminded when you have two feet of work piled up on your desk and he has two *actual* feet on his.

602 REASONS TO BE TICKED OFF

Getting arraigned the morning after the company Christmas party.

■

Staggering into the house crying with a cardboard box filled with desk supplies, a pink slip, and some unemployment forms and your lame-brained family asking, "What did the boss say about a raise?"

MAILMEN

602 REASONS TO BE TICKED OFF

Bubbly mailmen trying to strike up a friendship instead of just completing their mindless tasks and getting the hell off your front deck.

■

Watching the mailman pet your dog and wondering why on earth the animal isn't mauling the rancorous pinhead the way you trained him to.

Mailmen acting like miserable creeps the entire year, then becoming nice guys near Christmas hoping for a tip, as if you haven't seen that move a thousand times by every other phony douche bag in town.

■

☞ WHAT TO DO: ☜

Come out of the house with an envelope and wish the back-aching ding-a-ling a Merry Christmas. Hand him the envelope and say, "There's a check in there." After he offers up his phony thanks say, "What are you thanking me for? I just need you to mail that thing to the cable company. Now, hurry along before my dog devours your left ass cheek!"

Miserable mailguys who bitch about their job, then when they get fired and should be exulting in their freedom, instead decide to pull out a revolver and start shooting every mailbox and human being in sight.

◼

When the price of stamps keeps going up while the likelihood of your mail getting to its destination continues to plummet.

The pathetically wide counters at post offices across America that make it really difficult to reach across and slap a beating on these despicable wretches.

◼

Deplorable sorry-assed postal pinheads sighing and moaning behind the counter as if they're being asked to haul bricks and mix cement back there.

◼

Perverted postmen salaciously asking if you prefer your stamps "prelicked."

The mail arriving all shredded and torn, but since there are sufficient stamps on it, the post office has been paid in full so what the hell do they care?

WHAT TO DO:

Get back at your abysmal carrier by moving your mailbox to a new location every day until he has a nervous breakdown. Example: When the mailman pulls up to your box, remove it from the post and say, "I've decided to attach it to the house. Give me a hand holding the screws." The next day post a sign where the mailbox was with an arrow pointing to the backyard. Make sure the lid is glued shut. The next day, open an upstairs window and when he walks up the driveway, drop the metal box on his head and yell, "Nice job finding it!"

602 REASONS TO BE TICKED OFF

Mail coming back to you stamped "undeliverable" five years after you sent it—as if those hostile crudbags actually spent half a decade trying to deliver it.

■

Mail coming back to you stamped "Address not found," when it should actually read "Address never even looked for."

■

Mail coming back to you stamped "Forwarding address information not available," when it should say "I ain't busting my ass for no thirty-seven cents."

Mail coming back to you stamped "More postage needed," because it was off by one puny cent, and knowing if you happened to put four hundred extra stamps on an envelope you wouldn't get a dime back from those tightfisted maggots.

■

Forking over an extra two bucks for "Delivery Confirmation," because apparently placing a stamp in the right corner of the envelope doesn't guarantee you a damn thing anymore.

602 REASONS TO BE TICKED OFF

Continuing to get the previous resident's mail half a century after he moved out, and the future resident's mail a decade before they move in.

■

Telling the post office to stop delivering while you're away, then arriving home to a busted mailbox on the ground next to thirty pounds of weather-beaten packages.

IDIOTS

602 REASONS TO BE TICKED OFF

When you order cable TV installation and the customer service idiot says, "We'll be out there on a Monday sometime in the spring, fall, or winter so make sure you're home to let us in."

■

Mullet-headed cable repairmen who do such a discreet job of installing that you have a gaping hole in the roof, and a thick black wire duct-taped to the wall of every room in the house.

**Inane radio deejays who go on and on
about their lame weekend with their
goofy kids, while your favorite song
plays inaudibly in the background.**

Trying to show a dimwit how to program a
VCR and him looking at you like you're
asking him to disassemble it and then put
it back together blindfolded.

Slimeballs who, instead of saying, "Excuse me," after a series of burps, continue on talking as if, "Braaaaaaph, Uuuuuuuurp, and Waaaaaaak" are part of the sentence.

Making out with someone who fails
to tell you that they are about to puke.

■

Giving a bum some money just to shut
him up, but then he starts spouting wisdom
as if anyone has ever gained insight from
some irascible vermin who lives inside
a cardboard box and hasn't seen a roll
of toilet paper in three decades.

■

Homeless potbellied putzes who
stand around in Armani sweatsuits
listening to the latest CDs as they
beg for a crust of bread.

602 REASONS TO BE TICKED OFF

Dumping a whole bunch of change into some destitute clown's coffee cup, then later seeing the deceitful lout climbing behind the wheel of a fully loaded '98 Mustang.

■

Vile, shameless bums who claim to be war vets so you'll give them some drinking money, when all they have to do is go down to the VFW and drink for free with a bunch of other lushes who never saw a battlefield in their entire lives.

Getting lost and nearly killed trying to find someone's house because the street and stop signs were down, then later when you finally arrive and the dolt is giving you the tour, you see both signs nailed to his bedroom wall.

■

Horrendously ugly wretches who demand that you "Look right at me when I'm talking to you."

■

People with bad breath who get right in your face when they talk, as if it's important that you smell the words along with hearing them.

602 REASONS TO BE TICKED OFF

Halitosis-ridden scumbuckets who always seem to launch into one of their stench-ridden tales when they have you backed into a corner.

■

After telling the addle-brained butcher to slice the cheese fairly thin, the ham-head cuts it so thin it congeals together and becomes the thickest piece of cheese in history.

Stench-breathed fools who don't take
the hint when you offer them a mint every
two minutes and then ask, "Are you sure?"
as you point directly at their mouth and
then at your ass.

WHAT TO DO:

*Try to discreetly flick the mints into their
mouth as they are talking. If you manage to
get one into his tooth-decayed hole of death,
quickly challenge the skank to a contest to see
who can go the longest without swallowing.*

602 REASONS TO BE TICKED OFF

Some imbecile popping a champagne bottle at a party and sending the cork whizzing into your eye socket.

■

Inconsiderate pinheads holding funeral services on a Saturday, as if you have no better way to spend a weekend than to stand around a rotting, makeup-covered corpse shooting the breeze with a cabal of histrionic fools.

■

Some wafflehead bringing you to a party, then leaving you standing in a sea of babbling strangers who want absolutely nothing to do with you.

People deserting you at a party, then coming back to get you in the wee hours of the morning asking, "Wasn't that fun?" when you're still standing in the exact same spot in a now-vacant room.

■

Scummy vermin who converge on accident scenes with camcorders and start zooming in on injured people's faces as they wail for help.

When you start to tell a humorous story and some greedy attention-grabbing nipplehead cuts you off and finishes it for the big laugh.

Exaggerating a story to make it more
exciting, then realizing the people you're
talking to were all there when it happened
and are also well aware that you weren't.

**The procrastinating mullet-head who
comes in late for a movie and proceeds
to sit on thirty people before finally
lodging his ass in your popcorn bucket.**

602 REASONS TO BE TICKED OFF

Greasy, lip-smacking slobs who think the movie theater is their own private kitchen where they can boisterously shovel in salty treats and Pop Rocks as if they just spent four days in a Russian bread line.

■

Stupid moviegoing jackasses whispering during the previews, and deciding it's time to converse at a normal pitch when the movie starts.

Fat-gummed heinous mouths who wear braces and don't know enough to keep their magnetic, elasticized traps shut.

■

Trying to maintain your dignity as you walk around your hometown carrying steaming hot dog shit in a clear sandwich bag.

■

Walking through a public park and having to hopscotch over piles and piles of steaming hot dog crap.

---

602 REASONS TO BE TICKED OFF

Deceptively fraudulent phony-assed dog owners who walk around with sandwich bags that never seem to have any shit in them.

■

Pain-in-the-ass neighbors constantly asking you to "Give me a hand with this."

Dog owners who walk their filthy mutts over to your house so they can shit on your lawn.

 # WHAT TO DO:

Some people suggest taking your dog over to shit on their lawn. How amateur. Dog owners are not offended by dog crap. Walk over to their house and take the shit yourself, only don't put it on their lawn—deposit it on their dog. Then walk away with an empty plastic bag in your hand.

602 REASONS TO BE TICKED OFF

Looking at photos and some dolt telling you not to touch them with your fingers, as if you're somehow supposed to flip them with your frigging toes.

■

Utter fools who constantly say, "What," not because they didn't hear you, but rather because they need several extra seconds for the question to be absorbed by their microscopic brains.

■

Complete ding-a-lings who forget your name every damn time they see you.

Ignorant half-wits who insist they remember your name, and then finally guessing it after fifty-nine tries as they say, "See, I never forget."

■

Overweight parents who let their soon-to-be-humongous kids gorge on the same malnutritious waste they do.

■

Dumping someone and telling them, "It's really over this time," then having to crawl back five minutes later after exhausting your only other option.

602 REASONS TO BE TICKED OFF

Trying to get back together with someone you broke up with a month ago and finding out they're already pregnant and living with some other crudbag.

■

Barrel-chested pea brains who, instead of verbally describing a fight, have to physically demonstrate what they did to the other guy by punching you silly and then chucking you off a balcony.

Feebleminded mulyaks giving you
the tour of their studio apartments,
as if you don't see everything when
you bust open the front door.

■

Decrepit morons inviting you over to their
houses to watch the big game on four-inch
black-and-white TVs.

■

Skuzzbags borrowing your novels,
then returning them with notes in the
margins and yellow highlighter marks
all over the place.

Mushbrains borrowing a book and reading it in a steaming hot tub, then returning it as if you're ever going to be able to peruse the mildewed stack of deformed pulp again.

Total asses returning a book after two years and then informing you that, "I only read the first four pages."

■

Total scumbag neighbors taking so long to return your stuff they forget it's yours and say, "If I'm not using it and you need to borrow it, just let me know."

■

Never getting the chance to jump your neighbor from behind and beat him senseless with your shoe.

602 REASONS TO BE TICKED OFF

Dimwitted klutzheads who stand right in front of a TV and fiddle with the antenna when the reception was already perfect to begin with.

■

Turning on a TV and having your eardrums blown out because the volume is already cranked from the last deaf numbskull who used it.

■

Watching TV with some deaf old wretch who has the volume up so loud the picture tube explodes.

Waiting for the scrolling preview menu to arrive at the program you want to see, then by the time it does the frigging show is over.

Being unable to take control of someone else's TV because the clown has sixteen different remotes and not one of them has the word *television* on it.

Dropping your drunken friend off at 2 a.m. and having the cirrhosis-ridden lushbag call you an hour later to see if you want to head out for a few drinks.

602 REASONS TO BE TICKED OFF

Picking up some blockhead to go on a trip, and the ass saying, "First I have to go to the bank, grocery store, and cleaners, then we'll need to swing back here so I can take a quick leak and a nap."

■

Watching a mental-defective with sunblisters on his lips walk into your house and start drinking straight from the pitcher.

Complete airheads whipping into a space at the mall and sending a cavalcade of shopping carriages smashing into your vehicle, then getting out, looking at the carriages, and saying, "People are frigging idiots."

■

Trying to play a game of tennis and dodging balls from the physically impaired nimrods in the next court who keep lining felt balls at your head and then encourage each other by saying, "That was a close shot."

602 REASONS TO BE TICKED OFF

Backing up fifty feet thinking you have a parking spot and finding some chucklehead lying in the street holding it for a car he expects to be arriving sometime within the hour.

■

 WHAT TO DO:

Shout out the window, "You didn't have to go through all this trouble for me." Then park your car on top of this foolish maggot. Most likely he'll move, but if it's your lucky day you'll hear a crunch and loud screams, which should drown out the passengers inquiring, "Is there a guy under us?"

Hiking with some half-breed who
manages to bend every branch back so
it whips you across the face.

**Cretins who think their banal life
story is a proper response to the
question, "Hi, how are you today?"**

Asinine mourners who bawl and wail at a
funeral for a guy who lived over a century.

602 REASONS TO BE TICKED OFF

Guests who say, "We should get going now," but three hours later their asses are still buried in your sofa.

 # WHAT TO DO:

Pretend you're at their house. Grab your coat and say, "Well, I think it's time I took off. I never should have stayed this long, but you know how much of a rude bastard I can be. Always wearing out my welcome. I have got to learn to shut the hell up. Thanks for having me. Great house by the way!" Then drive off in their car and head over to their house. When they pull up in a cab shortly thereafter, say, "Did I leave something at your house, or are you just paying me a visit?"

Procrastinating boobs who show up several hours late and say, "Let's get right down to business cuz I'm in a real hurry."

602 REASONS TO BE TICKED OFF

Nimrod vegetarians who bring tofu to your cookout, as if you have time to flip soybean cakes when you're sucking down vodka gimlets and serving up dead-cow patties to a pack of plastered carnivores.

■

 # WHAT TO DO:

When the emaciated vegan arrives, hand him a bag of charcoal, a spatula, and directions to the nearest grill outlet. Tell him, "When you get back we'll all be wasted and having sex on the lawn in our mink underwear."

Kissing someone and mentioning that the birthmark on their lip is sexy, and hearing them reply, "Oh thanks, but it's herpes."

Trying to discreetly pass the pharmacy cashier some medicine, and the addled ninny yells to his coworkers, "How much do I charge this itchy bastard for the crab medicine?"

Sending your dingbat child to a major college and then grad school, after which the freaking klutz moves home and gets a job delivering supermarket circulars.

602 REASONS TO BE TICKED OFF

Semiretarded cluckheads who squeeze their automobiles into a seemingly impossible spot, so now *you* can't get in your damn car.

■

Eating a meal next to a total mullethead who, instead of asking politely for something to be passed, chooses to lean across the table so his elbow is in your temple and he's mashing your potatoes with his pelvis.

Driving back and forth over the gas station hose seventy-six times while the deaf attendant just sits there watching TV in his snack hut, completely oblivious to the loud bell ringing directly over his empty skull.

Feebleminded pus-heads in front of you who reverse their vehicles and then forget to put them back in drive, so when the light changes, you wind up in a neck brace drinking liquid pork through a crevice in your head cast.

Dialing the wrong number and the wack job on the other end wants to talk to you anyway.

602 REASONS TO BE TICKED OFF

Some nitwitted cluckhead calling you and asking what time you close, and after you tell him it's a residence, he yells, "Let me to speak to your boss!"

■

Muckle brains who call your house and ask for Fred, and after you tell the clueless fool, "There's no Fred here, ya moron," he says, "Well, who's this?" as if knowing your name is somehow gonna help him locate Fred.

Lunkheads dialing the wrong number, then calling back six more times hoping the person they're looking for just moved in.

Your old man smacking you around "to knock some sense into you," despite the wealth of medical evidence suggesting cranial damage does not lead to higher mental ability.

■

Antisocial dingbats who walk around with headphones on 24/7 and wonder why they don't have a solitary friend on the entire planet.

Going to a concert with your family and the drugged-out hippie at the end of the row keeps passing needles and lines of powder to your wife and kids.

Novels written by numbskulls in which you constantly have to go back several hundred pages to figure out things, like why some guy you thought died is now setting sail for America in a bathtub.

602 REASONS TO BE TICKED OFF

Uncoordinated Caucasian imbeciles who, believing they can dance, proceed out on the floor and set the progress of the white man back a couple of epochs.

■

Imbecilic athletic trainers dragging you off the field by the body part that you distinctly told him was broken.

■

Drowning and having some stupid, muscle-bound lifeguard with a brain the size of a testicle zing an eighty-pound life preserver with such force that it clanks off your head and knocks you unconscious.

Drowning while some mental-defective lifeguard sits on a big white chair mashing his mouth up against the zinc-coated lips of a 14-year-old bimbo.

■

Taking a dump in the sea, then quickly swimming away from the area straight into some other inconsiderate bastard's waste.

602 REASONS TO BE TICKED OFF

Knowing that lifeguards have to climb down a rickety ladder in bare feet before they can even enter the water, as if you got all the time in the world out there when you're drowning and getting devoured by sharks.

■

Bringing your sex-stained clothes to the cleaners and being asked by the dimwitted moron sniffing the stains, "How did these get here, and what exactly are they?"

Taking a trip with a guy who wants you to pull over and let him pee, smoke, and grab something to eat every six miles.

Your television antenna falling off your roof halfway through the Super Bowl.

602 REASONS TO BE TICKED OFF

Doctors talking so loud everyone in the waiting room and out in the hallways hears about your diarrhea, hemorrhoids, and impotence.

■

 **WHAT TO DO:**

Yell stuff back at him. "Okay, Doctor, I'll take that to get rid of my impotence. You say it worked for you, but only when you put on your mother's clothes and watched lots of gay porn, correct?"

Cutting your Adam's apple shaving
and watching three quarts of blood
go spurting into the sink.

People asking you if you're okay when
you're lying on the ground next to a
large sliver of your brain.

Taking your seventy-year-old mother
out to a comedy club for her birthday,
and the idiot on stage delivering a
forty-minute monologue on vaginas.

115

602 REASONS TO BE TICKED OFF

The knowledgeable man who did the job
estimate sending over two half-retarded
mutants to do the work.

■

Hiring people to do work by the hour
and coming home to an empty fridge
and a bunch of fat workers belly
flopping in your pool.

■

Playing chess and losing your queen
on the second move.

Playing chess with some halfwit who mulls over the board for three hours before making his opening move.

Spending three agonizing hours trying to checkmate some elusive bastard using only a knight and a bishop, then looking in the corner and seeing that your own king has been checkmated by a pawn.

602 REASONS TO BE TICKED OFF

After spending thirty bucks for a contour pillow because the ad says it "contours to the shape of your head" realizing every pillow does that unless you happen to be sleeping on a bag of cement.

■

Getting sucked in to paying thousands of dollars for an adjustable bed so you "can sit up and watch TV," then realizing that when you saw the commercial you were sitting in a regular flat bed watching frigging TV.

COPS

602 REASONS TO BE TICKED OFF

Cops complaining how stressful their jobs are, yet every time you see one he's pulled over to the side of the road shooting the breeze with another lard-ass cop or he's climbing back into the front seat naked as a hooker escapes through the alley.

■

Buffoonish cops pulling off to the breakdown lane to chat, as if that's not gonna cause a ten-mile backup.

Getting ready to make love in the backseat of your car but a highway safety officer shows up and tells you to move it along, as if the roads are somehow "safer" with sexually pent-up drivers frantically racing around town searching for a hiding spot.

■

Dingbatted cops writing up a ticket in the time it takes most people to pen an epic novel.

Numbingly impersonal police stations that have plexiglass up like we're a bunch of diseased crackheads, so you have to stoop down like a hunchback and shout into a two-inch porthole to some bung-breathed jackass who stands nowhere near the hole and screams, "Ya gotta speak up, fuzznuts."

■

Going down to the cop station to obtain a gun license and the brain-dead chumps have the audacity to ask you why you need a gun, as if their penchant for whaling people with clubs and spraying errant bullets all over the damn place isn't reason enough.

Police officers putting on great displays of integrity by publicly blowing through stop signs, stumbling into bars and strip joints, and uttering antidrug lectures in the middle of three-day acid trips.

Getting your ass kicked in a parking lot while a lieutenant watches from the car during his coffee break.

602 REASONS TO BE TICKED OFF

Bellowing your head off at a cop as he walks back to your car after a forty-minute delay, then staring in disbelief as he rips up the warning slip and heads back to his car to write you a ticket.

■

Blind cops shining a flashlight in your eyes as they approach your car, as if your vehicle isn't already illuminated by their high beams and the multicolored disco ball twirling on their roof.

Numbskulled police officers using the term, "Write you up a ticket," as if it takes some kind of literary genius to copy down a plate number and three digits off a radar gun.

WHAT TO DO:

When he hands you the ticket tell him, "This looks really well written. I can't wait to get home and read it. Nothing I like better than to curl up next to a fire with a good ticket. I think I read one of yours before. It was about a guy who blows through a red light, doesn't pay the fine, and gets his license revoked. This must be the sequel. Oh, and you gave me a signed copy. Thanks, Porky."

602 REASONS TO BE TICKED OFF

Waking up the neighborhood getting pulled over by multiple cop cars in front of your house, then having them peek into your vehicle and call for the SWAT unit, two packs of drug-sniffing dogs, a bomb team, and fourteen fire trucks.

■

Trying to run away with handcuffs on and falling flat on your face five feet from where you initially took off.

Utterly dumb cops barking, "Step out of the car," into a megahorn when they're standing right outside your window that they just smashed to pieces with a club.

602 REASONS TO BE TICKED OFF

When you're *completely sober* but so nervous during a field sobriety test you can't walk a straight line, and then you try your hand at the alphabet and somehow end up forgetting sixteen of the letters.

■

The hypocrisy of getting a ticket for a broken directional light that was written by a cop who hasn't signaled for a turn since he took his driver's test back in high school.

Lugheaded cops leaving the flashing lights on the whole time, just in case anybody wasn't sure which vehicle was the cop car.

■

Cops parking fifty yards behind you, so along with waiting for the pinhead to write the ticket, you also have to sit idly by while he walks his misshapen body over a lengthy stretch of pavement in six-foot-high hooker boots.

602 REASONS TO BE TICKED OFF

Some moronic cop using the jaws of life to get you out of a car and snipping both your legs off with the massive hedge clippers.

■

The hypocrisy of getting a ticket for "driving to endanger" by a cop who had to go 140 mph down a sidewalk in reverse in order to catch you.

Hypocritical cops citing the potential for testicular cancer from leaving radar guns in their laps, but thinking nothing of firing the tumor-causing musket at our families' brains as we whiz by them on the highway.

Cops acting all generous by saying, "I'll let you off with a warning this time," when they really mean, "I'm out of tickets, you lucky bastard," or "I think I'm correct but I don't feel like flipping through a stack of law books right now."

Corpulent desk cops who answer the phone with a surly attitude, as if you're the one who stuffed 300,000 glazed doughnuts down his oversized gullet over a ten-year period.

■

Cops blasting us for overblowing the whole cop–doughnut thing by pointing out that the white powder on their lips is sometimes not confectionary sugar, but rather the residue from snorting confiscated crack or heroin.

TICKED OFF ABOUT COPS

Idiotically falling for the "good cop–bad cop" routine, when it's so obviously fake because there is no such thing as a good cop.

■

Undercover cops getting all pissed when you play their game by zipping down the street at night with your headlights off and your license plate tucked in the glovey.

■

Events that have an auxiliary cop on duty, as if they're not the first ones out the door as soon as any hair-raising shit goes down.

602 REASONS TO BE TICKED OFF

Cops who sit in their cars all day laughing
at old broads trying to go up one-ways
the wrong way and entering DO NOT ENTER
areas, then when you try the same thing
they swoop in and beat you halfway to
stupidity with a tire iron.

■

Cops who confiscate your dope,
smoke it, and tell you it's the best
they've ever had.

Sitting on the side of the road waiting for an addled cop to write you a speeding ticket, while motorists with hostages gagged in the front seat go whizzing by at 188 mph firing off shotguns, smoking joints, and chucking empty vodka bottles out the window.

■

Getting cited for drinking and driving by a cop who can't even stand erect.

602 REASONS TO BE TICKED OFF

Arrogant U.S. police departments expecting you to crawl out of the wreckage and draw a diagram of your car accident on the police report, as if you can remember anything after sucking down a vat of gin and plowing into the side of a mountain.

■

Foolishly allowing cops to talk you into taking the breathalyzer test, then blowing into the tube and setting a new station record on the damn machine.

TOLLS
AND
DRIVING

602 REASONS TO BE TICKED OFF

After making your nightly drive right past the toll basket without paying, and hearing the familiar bell go off, it's now followed by a not-so-familiar siren.

■

Arrogant toll collectors getting all huffy when you don't have exact change, as if you're supposed to drive around with a coin vault in your backseat.

■

Paranoid toll collectors wearing latex gloves and acting as if you're a syphilis patient handing them a urine specimen.

Driving through the new automated toll system and all these stupid lights and buzzers go off just because you never bothered signing up for the damn thing.

■

WHAT TO DO:

As you approach the automated toll, look for another vehicle that has the automatic transponder attached to the windshield. Then get right on his bumper and go through as his guest.

The fact that toll collectors are up high so they can glare down on drivers, when these blue-collar idiots deserve to be working in six-foot pits whereupon we could dump money, pour out trash, and relieve our jammed-up bowels on their heads.

■

Toll collectors spending five minutes giving driving directions to some lost fool, as if one lost guy is more important than the five hundred people who are now going to be suspended, fired, or castrated by their spouses.

Requesting a receipt from the uneducated sap in the toll booth and he looks at you like you just ordered him to wax the undercarriage of your vehicle.

602 REASONS TO BE TICKED OFF

Completely insane states that have five-lane highways suddenly converge on a single toll booth that's being operated by a mentally impaired nimrod who should be hauled out back and beaten with a cash register.

■

When you take the wrong exit on a toll road and to avoid paying extra money, you end up doing an illegal U-turn and driving down the highway with fourteen cones wedged beneath your vehicle.

Pinheaded toll maggots who say, "Ya got anything smaller?" after you hand them a bill, as if they have to get in their car and drive across town to the bank to change the damn thing.

■

WHAT TO DO:

Point at their brain and ask, "Don't you have anything bigger?"

602 REASONS TO BE TICKED OFF

Insolent toll guys who won't accept a personal check for forty-five cents.

■

 # WHAT TO DO:

If you sense an attitude from the toll collector as he sticks his hand out for the money, say, "Sorry, pal, but I'm going to need both hands cupped." Then hand him a ceramic pig. "Hold onto this while I smash it with a hammer. And ya better turn that red light on above your vacant skull cuz we're gonna be here awhile."

Simpletons who pay no heed to the three-car explosion they just caused in their selfish haste to get over to the passing lane.

Driving a non-air-conditioned vehicle that is so hot you have to blast the heater to stay cool.

Realizing that your automobile rolled down a hill and killed a boatload of people.

602 REASONS TO BE TICKED OFF

People who put CAUTION: BLIND DRIVEWAY signs up, as if the people driving by should be careful because this total dingbat purchased himself the shittiest house on the planet.

■

☞ WHAT TO DO: ☜

Make a sign and put it in his driveway so when he pulls out he sees: CAUTION! CARS WHIZZING BY.

■

Hopping out of your car and realizing it's still in drive and heading straight for some gas pumps.

Some frighead friend saying, "Follow me in your car," and then proceeding to motor through a school zone at 96 mph.

■

After seeing four mammoth signs telling you that your exit is approaching you still miss it.

■

Morons borrowing your car then returning it with the seat so far up you can't get in, the mirrors angled down at the floorboards, and all your tapes and CDs fried to a crisp on the dashboard.

602 REASONS TO BE TICKED OFF

After you blast your horn at a stupid-ass driver, some massive bastard gets out, so you quickly jerk the wheel to the right, pin the pedal to the floor, and unexpectedly run out of gas.

■

Getting pulled out of your vehicle and beaten to a pulp at a red light as fifty other drivers cheer and shout violent suggestions.

■

A cop pulling up, witnessing another driver assaulting you, and deciding to give him a hand.

Getting stuck behind some cowardly driver who apparently can't pull out onto the road unless there are no cars visible anywhere along the horizon.

602 REASONS TO BE TICKED OFF

Sitting in traffic for three hours because nosy humans need to glare at bent fenders and corpses impaled on steering columns.

■

Driving past a GASOLINE THIS EXIT sign, then seeing a sign that says NEXT EXIT 200 MILES and then another that says NEXT GAS 400 MILES.

■

When the automatic "safety" buckle comes up and smacks you in the temple, then the belt wraps around your neck and chokes you.

Pulling in on the wrong side of the gas pump, then brilliantly pulling around to the other side so your tank is still on the wrong side.

◼

Shrewdly trying to yank the fuel nozzle over the top of your car instead of moving the vehicle, thus scraping the hell out of your paint job and pumping fifty cents' worth of gas into your trunk.

602 REASONS TO BE TICKED OFF

Doing all the driving on a road trip, and the only one who even offers to take over is some drunken, tobacco-chewing cokehead with a patch over one eye who keeps saying, "I hope we crash."

■

When a stupid nimrod breaks down in the middle of the road but doesn't put his hazards on, so you sit behind him for half an hour wondering what the hell the delay is all about.

Leaving the gas station and hearing the sound of your tires crushing your gas cap.

Waiting for some incompetent dingbat to parallel park in a space they could have pulled straight into.

Feeble-minded buffoons who say, "I'm really good at parallel parking," as if a skill that is accomplished daily by every kind of maladroit imaginable deserves some kind of worldwide recognition.

602 REASONS TO BE TICKED OFF

People who tell you how good they are at parallel parking, then you sit in the car and suffer whiplash as they lurch back and forth trying to shoehorn an Expedition into a spot reserved for compacts.

■

Foolish mulyaks who drive your car and say, "I'll fit it in that spot," and three broken taillights later they point at the badly angled car that's destined for a tow and say, "See."

Picking up your car at the tow-truck joint and there's the added bonus of a parking ticket pinned to your cracked windshield.

■

Celebrating because you didn't get towed out of an illegal spot, then trying to drive off and realizing you can't because there's a giant steel boot on your tire.

■

Having your key break off in the lock, so you smash the window with a rock, hop in, and then discover it isn't your car.

Asking the brainless dunce at the tow-truck yard to show you where your car is, and he points to a vehicle that is being dropped to the earth by a crane and says, "That'll be fifty bucks."

Trying to drive across a street but your view is blocked by a van, so its driver takes a peek and waves you right into the flammable section of an oil tanker.

■

As you're attempting to check the spark plugs in your car, some idiot jumps in and fires up the engine.

■

Having a cop follow you for ten miles making you so nervous you zigzag all over the road knocking down mailboxes and plowing over small road signs.

602 REASONS TO BE TICKED OFF

Lazy nitwits who don't clean off the tops of their cars after snow storms, and are completely oblivious when a glacier slab slides off their roof, smashes to smithereens on your windshield, and causes you to veer off into a frozen lake.

■

Driving through a completely empty parking lot with a total moron who keeps pointing out the open spots and questioning your ability to drive.

Wise-ass pedestrians who slam the back of your car with their hand and then limp away as if you hit them.

WHAT TO DO:

Get out of the car and pretend you really did hit the person by grabbing them around the neck and saying, "I gotta get you to a doctor." Chuck the moron into the back seat and quickly feel for a pulse. Begin pummeling his chest with your fists and start yelling, "Clear! Oh, gosh, I'm losing him!" Then whack him in the face a bunch of times before leaving him bleeding by the roadside as you drive off "to go get help."

---

602 REASONS TO BE TICKED OFF

After reading off a two-page order for a vanload of your malnourished junk-food-addict friends at the drive-through window, you hear the headset-wearing pustule face inside say, "Welcome to Burger Hut, may I take your order, please?"

■

Fast-food-serving zit faces asking, "Do you want fries with that?" when you just ordered ten boxes of the coagulated spud strips.

Lazy lunks flipping out after you've parked, because you easily could have torn the paint off your car wedging into a space that was two spots closer to the building.

Asking a nervous passenger to hold the steering wheel while you jot something down, then looking up and discovering you're in mid air plummeting toward a gravel pit.

602 REASONS TO BE TICKED OFF

Some asinine zit head driving off in the car that you were underneath working on.

■

When you're already doing at least forty miles over the speed limit and some zipperhead behind you gives you the high beams, apparently because you don't have *flames* shooting out of your tailpipe.

■

Ramming into the back of a car because you were trying to read a bumper sticker that says HIT ME, I NEED THE MONEY.

When you barely tap the fender of another car and the phony driver falls out his door and starts clutching his neck, back, and ass.

■

When you're in the back of an ambulance heading to the hospital in an emergency situation and the halfwit EMT in the passenger seat tells the driver to, "Slow down. This isn't a race!"

602 REASONS TO BE TICKED OFF

Overly cautious lardbutts pressing the WALK button when there are no cars around for miles, so by the time you drive up, you still have to stop and watch him haul his gargantuan ass safely across the street.

■

When you're up late watching television and some drunken mullet-head comes smashing into your living room.

■

Hurting your foot while trying to land several looping roundhouse kicks to some bloody intruder's mangled-up face.

After you finish giving driving directions over the phone to some imbecile, he says, "Can you repeat those? I'm going to grab a pen and write them down this time."

■

 **WHAT TO DO:**

When he says, "I have a pen, go ahead," tell him, "Okay, what you do is get in the car and run a hose from the exhaust pipe into the window. Then when you start to feel all disoriented, floor that gas pedal. You'll know you've arrived when you're beeping the horn with your head.

602 REASONS TO BE TICKED OFF

Deranged scar-faced lunatics who sit in the passenger seat and bellow, "You can make this light," when you're six hundred feet from it and it's yellow.

■

Being forced to order a pizza using your expensive cell phone, because some inconsiderate cluckhead just cut off your residential service seconds ago by smashing into a telephone pole in front of your house.

Corrupt politicians who pass mandatory seat belt laws while they drunkenly tool around D.C. unbuckled in their Mercedes, slamming into parked cars and trees.

Jerking the steering wheel back and forth in your car horsing around, and ending up killing a whole slew of people.

602 REASONS TO BE TICKED OFF

Pulling way too far forward into a parking spot and crashing through the window of a supermarket.

■

WHAT TO DO:

Play it off like you meant it. Hop out and say, "You guys are open, right? Is it all right if I park there, or should I pull forward into the cracker aisle?"

■

Driving an overly safe car designed by a pack of pussified engineers and lightly tapping someone's fender, which causes your seat belt to lock you up in a Texas choke hold and the air bag to pop out and suffocate your poor helpless ass.

Trying to quickly speed away from an accident scene but your car won't start because it's engulfed in flames.

■

When you torch your car for insurance and some imbecile calls the fire department and for once in their failed history the rubber-jacketed pinheads arrive in time.

■

Peabrains who can afford to drive right up your ass because the front of their car is already pulverized beyond repair.

602 REASONS TO BE TICKED OFF

Driving around in a burnt-out smelly minivan because your insurance fraud scheme didn't go so well.

170

TICKED OFF ABOUT | TOLLS AND DRIVING

Intentionally smashing up your crapbox real good, then having some asinine insurance clown pull up in a dented lime green Pinto, look over your heap of mangled steel, and say, "Looks okay to drive to me."

When four highway lanes merge down to one in the middle of rush-hour traffic cuz the road department is a cabal of tar-inhaling alcoholic morons, then the one lane gets pinched in with cones so you have to get up on two tires just to get through the frigging mishmash.

602 REASONS TO BE TICKED OFF

Skidding to a stop at a traffic light that holds on yellow for ten seconds, so you cockily cruise through the next yellow light only to have it quickly turn red as you slide across an intersection and smash into a mailbox.

■

Successfully lying your way out of a car accident, then spying some geeky pinhead showing the cops a videotape of you blowing through a stop sign, colliding with five cars, and then claiming someone else was driving your car.

When an addled driver takes a left turn at an intersection and waves thanks for letting him cut in front of you, when in fact you still have a red light and would have given your right arm for the chance to send this dink swan diving out his passenger-side window.

■

Cowards who sprint away from a fiery car wreck with their CD collection and a bag of Fritos before the vehicle explodes, while you lie drenched with gasoline in the back seat screaming, "HELP!"

602 REASONS TO BE TICKED OFF

After pulling over to pick up a hitchhiker, all of a sudden seven other thugs come out of the bushes and hop in, too.

■

 # WHAT TO DO:

Tell them to hop right in. Then say, "Glad you all made it to the meeting point at the correct time. Now let's get our blindfolds on and proceed with the sacrifice of our lives to the supreme master."
As you place the cloth over your eyes, say, "Most likely, I'm going to drive over the cliffs around the next turn, but if the guardrail is too high, I got plenty of rifles in the trunk."
When you remove the cloth, you'll either be all alone, or there'll be one guy left who can easily be dropped off at the next bridge.

Lamebrained joggers continuing to run in place when you stop to ask them for directions, as if you can hear a word they're saying when their feet are scuffing the ground and they're sucking in air like they've had their head dunked in a toilet for five minutes.

■

Hitchhiking while people who know you toot the horn, wave, and drive right by.

Criminal-looking hitchhikers who give you a foul look when you don't pick them up two hundred feet from the entrance to the jail.

Arrogant hitchhiking nitwits who hop in your car and start readjusting the heater and turning on their favorite radio stations.

■

After picking up a hitchhiker in the middle of nowhere a news flash comes on the radio about motorists disappearing from the highway.

602 REASONS TO BE TICKED OFF

Asking some unkempt hitchhiker where he's going and he says, "Up the road a ways," as if your plan was to drive the scenic route through people's backyards.

■

Hitchhikers who hold up signs indicating what town they want to go to, while the important stuff like how many people they've hacked up is nowhere on the placard.

OLD
PEOPLE

602 REASONS TO BE TICKED OFF

Old rickety coots who are so desperate for your companionship that they continue yapping as they walk alongside your car while you futilely try to drive away.

◼

Trying to figure out the sixteen different locking mechanisms on some old lout's door so you can get the hell out of there before he wakes up.

◼

Paying some lackluster dullard a visit and you age seven years just listening to the total bore wax on about his shoes.

Old slugs saying, "I'll make a long story short," as you sit there wishing you could hear the long version because you've heard the short one sixty-seven frigging times.

■

Obsolescent crusty binnies shouting, "I won't stay long," and then you realize that someone who's been on earth for ninety years has an extremely different idea of "long."

602 REASONS TO BE TICKED OFF

Waking up from a nap to some old gray stokehole who's ranting about the same doctor's appointment he was droning on about when you nodded off.

■

When the signal light turns green but the idiotic slouched lizard in front of you has apparently decided to sit this cycle out.

■

Blasting your horn at some old cruster and instead of adjusting his atrocious driving, he adjusts his mirror so he can see "what's making all the racket back there."

Miserable acid-ridden coots complaining around the clock about everything from politics to the un-elasticity of their underwear.

Rancorous married couples constantly bitching at each other in public.

Paying pathetically high health, car, and life insurance rates cuz of all the ancient gizzards out there abusing their frail bodies, clogging up the roads, and dying in utterly mysterious ways.

Old buzzardy bastards
with money who
marry thirty-year-old
bombshells, leaving us
to pick from the heap
of eighty-year-old bats
they should have married.

Dumb-assed senior citizens insisting, "I don't need to live in a nursing home" as dung, piss, and gas gush out of every orifice in their body.

After tucking some grizzled relative into a nursing home so you can get on with your life, the noxious geezer is ringing your doorbell a mere two hours later thanks to the strict security at those dumps.

Fighting an old guy and dealing with the frustration of trying to exert just enough pressure to hold him down, but not so much that he expires.

602 REASONS TO BE TICKED OFF

Paranoid old crispy bastards who insist their grocery total is off by a nickel, so you give the lout five cents, which he pockets and then continues arguing about the nickel.

■

Stingy old gray heads who constantly tell the cashier that they have exact change, but never mention that it's scattered among six different pockets, two socks, and a burlap pouch they keep tucked in their underwear.

Retirees who look at the total on the cash register, then remember that they have several hundred thousand coupons, a senior discount card, and they need to get one more item in aisle Z along with a box of Depends and a small chicken.

Acrimonious old coots counting their loaded shopping carriage as one item and proceeding to frig up the day of ten innocent people who actually have jobs and lives.

602 REASONS TO BE TICKED OFF

Heinous-looking old cruds who smash into three automobiles backing out of a parking spot, then get out to survey the damage to *their* car before driving off.

■

Inconsiderate oldies ruining a great theater performance by having a heart attack during the love scene and then creating an even bigger stir by falling out of the balcony.

■

Foolish old ninnies putting around in expensive sports cars instead of hopping into wheelchairs where they belong.

Being dragged to a funeral for some 112-year-old hunk of dust, and the 114-year-old wife is bawling on your shoulder because it was "so sudden."

☞ WHAT TO DO: ☜

Perpetuate this miserable wretch's grief even more by bellowing in her wax-encrusted ear, "I wasn't expecting it either. What a shock! I mean, come on here! Next thing they'll be telling me is that you're dying. God works in mysterious ways, but this is totally ridiculous. Here today, gone a century and a decade plus two years later. We barely got to know the man. Is there no justice? I simply can't go on, can you?"

602 REASONS TO BE TICKED OFF

Showing up to a town meeting to ask one lousy question, but some old spot-covered lizard cuts you off and filibusters for three days about the temperature of his tap water.

◼

Incompetent senior citizens who take jobs as supermarket baggers so we customers have the pleasure of bringing overstuffed, broken-handled bags into our homes and then unloading a drool-coated pile of pummeled bread, mangled boxes, and pulverized fruit.

Deaf and dumbassed whiteheads who yell, "Speak up. I can't hear you," instead of, "I am too stubborn to get a hearing aid, plus I love shouting cuz I'm such a loud asswipe!"

■

Spending your own money on a hearing aid just so you can hook it up to your dust-ridden granddad and bellow "You gotta move out of here, you old sausage!"

■

Weather-beaten sun hags parading around half nude in silk thongs while the rest of us retch on our blankets.

602 REASONS TO BE TICKED OFF

Shaking some putrid old-timer's hand
and coming away with a palm full of
gunk you can't even identify.

■

When you're making really good time
getting to an important appointment and
some venomous old lout pulls in front of you
and changes the entire course of your life.

■

Tiny old people always feeling the
need to purchase the largest
automobiles ever made.

Beeping at some heinous wretch and he's so out of it he waves hello, as if a hello toot is ever a three-minute horn blast followed by a middle finger and a death-defying pass along the guardrail.

■

Old curly-toed couples who, despite a plethora of seats, decide to sit right next to you and describe every solitary nuance of the movie in their hoarse, scratchy voices.

602 REASONS TO BE TICKED OFF

Craggly old bastards who are mentally unable to make a deposit into their savings account without summoning the help of a branch manager, a team of loan officers, and sixteen security guards.

■

 # WHAT TO DO:

The bank should have a separate line for these silver-headed mulyaks. The teller should be at least eighty and be well-read in the handbook titled Simple Banking Transactions Made Painstakingly Difficult.

After the doctor gives you permission to pull the plug on some rich relative, you jerk the cord out of the machine, pop a bottle of champagne, and then discover that the shriveled lummox has undergone a miraculous recovery.

■

An old bat passing away seconds before she was about to sign all her belongings over to you.

■

Paying your distant aunt several last-minute visits to her sickbed and then not finding your name anywhere on the vindictive broad's will.

602 REASONS TO BE TICKED OFF

Sick relatives selfishly getting hooked up to some lifesaving machine and proceeding to suck every dime out of the family coffers.

■

Malevolent old bats who always seem to pass away right when you're stepping off the plane on some tropic isle.

WHAT TO DO:

When you answer the phone and they tell you so-and-so died, say, "Oh, you almost got me there, you sneaky bastard. I was about to hang up and book a flight home, but I can hear the quiver in your voice. You always crack under pressure when you're pulling these gags. See you in a couple of weeks." When you get home and they try to make you feel guilty by showing you the evidence, say, "Man, you guys went all out on this prank, huh? Burial notices in the paper, an invoice for a coffin, a gravestone with his name chiseled on it, and his wife all despondent in the corner. Hell, you guys probably have him stashed in some hole in the ground somewhere. Not bad, guys, not bad."

When some old wrinkly crudbag, who has been driving six mph for thirty minutes, suddenly kicks it up to 110 when you try to pass him on the left.

Old goats insisting they can still drive safely after smashing through their fourth storefront window in a week, in cars they mistakenly thought were their own.

Ancient maggots insisting they don't need a walker as they pitch head-first down the cellar stairs.

602 REASONS TO BE TICKED OFF

The prickheaded fools at the registry of motor vehicles making the roads a living hell by handing out license renewals to every gray-haired ninny that slaps thirty bucks on the counter and gets two out of fifteen letters right on the eye test.

■

Grandparents who are always jumping out of their seats because they think more people have arrived, despite the fact that everyone has already arrived *and* left.

Balding gray-haired sports announcers who can't even see the color commentator, never mind the tiny players down on the field.

■

Unctuous old vultures telling lame stories that end in, "You had to be there," as if that's possible when it happened nine decades ago.

■

Old men who smoke smelly pipes, as if these pleated maggots don't stink enough on their own.

602 REASONS TO BE TICKED OFF

Prehistoric golfers who spend fifteen minutes looking for their drive on the fairway and can't find it because they never even hit it.

Phoning an old relative and the machine picks up first, so you have to spend five minutes listening to the flummoxed nitwit fumbling around and muttering, "I wonder what this button does."

Old fogies who run upstairs to turn the answering machine off before talking to you, as if a recorded message between you and some old goat is going to fall into the wrong hands.

602 REASONS TO BE TICKED OFF

Hanging up from a conversation with an old relative and realizing all you said was, "Hello," and, "It was wonderful talking to you."

■

Timeworn bastards taking a short break from their oration on socks to say, "You're awfully quiet over there."

■

Primitive buzzards talking about the "good ol' days," which makes you feel like your life is a steaming pile of crap.

Putrid-looking coots harping about the "good ol' days," and always leaving out the part about two world wars, the Great Depression, and five out of every eight people dying from smallpox.

■

Saying "Bless you," after some wretch sneezes, then you sneeze twenty times while they look on in disgust.

■

Changing an old guy's diaper and trying to think back in your life to where it all went wrong.

602 REASONS TO BE TICKED OFF

Idiots who put ninety of those birthday candles that won't blow out on an old man's cake, so everyone gets dessert coated with a thin sheet of Grandpa's bacillus-ridden saliva.

■

Unbelievably stupid old bastards who lug an oxygen tank over to the stove so they can light their cigars.

■

Dumber than dumb old cragglers who find out their liver disease is improving and celebrate by whacking down a gallon of gin.

TICKED OFF ABOUT OLD PEOPLE

Forgetting your relative's nursing home room number, forcing you to search the halls while dodging puddles and getting attacked by eighty-year-old mumbling whack jobs.

Old louts constantly asking you to "speak up," when you haven't even said a word.

Trying to hold a conversation with a nursing home patient while simultaneously holding your breath.

602 REASONS TO BE TICKED OFF

Weak, retired oldies who frig up
an entire election because they don't
have the strength to poke a sharp
metal point through a piece of
perforated paper.

■

 WHAT TO DO:

*Change the laws. When you are eighteen you
are eligible to vote for your candidate. When
you turn seventy you will be tattooed on the
forehead with a picture of an empty hourglass
and subsequently stoned on sight if you so
much as approach a voting booth.*

Old politicians who are always trying to help the elderly get ahead, as if the elderly haven't already had close to a century to take care of that for themselves.

602 REASONS TO BE TICKED OFF

Ancient crusters accusing the
current generation of being selfish,
as they don mink coats and head
down to Florida in Lexus convertibles
carpeted with lambskin seats.

■

Gray-haired buzzards who insist their
Cadillacs be equipped with night-vision
windshields, despite the fact they haven't
been out past suppertime since 1975.

AIR
TRAVEL

602 REASONS TO BE TICKED OFF

Going into the communist-run airport snack shop for a quick snack and spending half your traveler's checks on a bag of chips.

■

The numbskulls working at the ticket desk who think they can make flying safer by simply asking every passenger if they have plans to hijack the plane.

■

Pompous putzes who hold up the boarding line of a flight so they can stuff the overhead bin with golf clubs, two scooters, and a grand piano.

When the overhead bin above your seat is completely crammed with shit that belongs to a scurrilous wretch who is sitting fifteen rows behind you.

Feckless-minded dipshits who immediately jump up to get their belongings the split second the plane arrives at the gate, despite the fact that they never get off any faster than people like me who just sit there laughing at them.

602 REASONS TO BE TICKED OFF

Looking in the captivating flight guide magazine and seeing that the same suckass film that will be shown going across the country will also be featured on the return flight, as well as any future flight you may be taking in the next decade.

■

Sappy airline attendants interrupting your hard drinking to ask if you want chicken or beef, as if all the meat isn't coming off the same carcass, which happens to be nothing even resembling a chicken or a cow.

Cheap airlines that pass out bags of peanuts that are labeled "Not for resale," which is painfully obvious because how could one possibly put a price on five sugared nuts?

■

Flight attendants wasting everyone's time giving some retarded safety lecture, as if a breathing mask is gonna save you when you're plowing into Mount Rushmore.

602 REASONS TO BE TICKED OFF

The well-thought-out system on airlines where you eat a wretched meal that goes through you in ten seconds, and then the suicide machine on wheels that brought you the bacterial stew is now blocking your path to the bathroom.

■

Sitting on a plane watching feature-length films on a calculator-sized movie screen that is conveniently located directly in line with the warped skull of the goon in front of you.

Paying four dollars for a set of headphones that you have to hold pinned against your head because the previous wearer had a cranium the size of a medicine ball.

When the pilot interrupts a crucial scene in the movie to tell you, "It's forty-six degrees in Tulsa," which is a key city because it's a mere two time zones from where you're eventually going to either land or crash.

Walking off the plane after yet another disastrous, rocky flight and the entire crew has the balls to stand there waiting for you to commend them.

Cowardly pilots who stay up in the cockpit after the flight so you don't get the opportunity to flip them the middle digit and tell them what a sucky job they did manning the craft.

Pressing the call button fifteen times and, sure enough, the mascara-covered space waitress never comes to your aid; then some wrinkled old wretch presses it once, and within seconds six attendants are breastfeeding and burping the chronic lout.

Screaming, wailing babies who get taken onboard by some ignoramus who apparently never heard of a muzzle or a tranquilizer gun.

■

Hypocritical attendants cutting you off from drinking alcohol when it's common knowledge that as soon as the plane lands, these pent-up broads run wild all over the city getting blitzed and sleeping with everyone in sight.

Flight attendants turning you down for a date with some illogical reason like "I don't date passengers," as if the bevy of strangers they sleep with on land all travel by helicopter.

■

Airport security dingbats who frisk you to death and force you to strip down to your undies, while thugs with "I hate America" T-shirts stroll right up to the gate with ticking briefcases and boots that have lit fuses sticking out of the heels.

602 REASONS TO BE TICKED OFF

W hen your $400 seat reclines only about two inches but the corpulent fat-ass numbskull in front of you is somehow able to drop his bald sweaty head in your lap.

F ighting over the armrest with some blowhard who has no idea the limits you'll go to obtain what is rightfully yours.

Utterly stupid lunkheads who say, "Have a safe flight," as if you have any control over this six hundred–foot luggage rack when you're seated eighty rows from the instrument panel.

■

WHAT TO DO:

Phone this brainless wonder when you're up in the sky and say, "I just wanted to let you know I'm having a safe flight. At one point I almost stormed the cockpit, then I remembered what you said about being safe. What a close call. I'd be dead if it wasn't for you."

602 REASONS TO BE TICKED OFF

The flight getting detoured to the nearest airport because some dunce tried to seize control of the plane with a knife that was fashioned from a stale brownie.

■

Unscrupulous lying bastards who claim to be members of the "Mile-High Club," when it's painfully obvious from their heinous appearance they're not even members of the extremely common "Sea-Level Club."

When the inebriated pinhead sitting next to you at the airport bar glances at your ticket and says he's on the same flight as you, only he'll be sitting in the cockpit.

Rich pompous crudbags who sit in first class and give you that smarmy look as you drunkenly stagger down the aisle toward the poverty-stricken coach section.

Listening to the tycoons up front sucking down champagne and eating lobster, while you stare at a plate of food that would draw boos at a homeless shelter.

Sitting next to some rank child whose parent decides to hold him with his rear orifice facing you the whole flight.

Sitting next to repugnant parents who tell their baby, "I'll change your diaper as soon as we land," as the plane lifts off the ground and heads overseas.

Sharing a seat on a plane with the excess dripping fat of the blubberneck who's sitting four seats over.

602 REASONS TO BE TICKED OFF

Tasting your own urine because you tried to piss when the plane was flying through turbulence.

■

Inept pilots constantly blaming turbulence for their inability to hold the steering wheel straight.

■

Paying ten bucks for a "glass of wine" as the attendant hands you a Dixie cup and a two-ounce can of fermented grapes that tastes like it was trod on by some fungal-footed Sicilian.

Nippleheaded airline attendants expecting you to tip them, when the bulk of the booze in your system is from the liquor you smuggled onboard.

Sitting on an airplane next to an airsick passenger who's presently filling his seventh barf bag.

Dingbats who keep playing with all the buttons above their seat so you get treated to a light show and a torrent of stale musty air sporadically blowing your hair all over the damn place.

When a pain-in-the-scrotum passenger with a bladder the size of a Brazil nut climbs over you to take a leak every five minutes, then you ask him to switch seats and the besotted pinhead says, as he parks his ass in your face yet again, "No thanks. I really don't mind climbing over."

∎

Nitwits asking you if you are waiting for the airline bathroom, as if your answer is going to be, "No, I just enjoy standing around losing my balance while the stench of other people's waste wafts up my nostrils."

Feebleminded cretins approaching the bathroom and saying, "Can I go next? I just have to pee," as if you've got diarrhea written all over your face.

■

Dumber-than-a-bowl-of-jello limo drivers awaiting you with a cardboard sign with your name chicken-scratched on it, as if any old pinhead can't just say, "I'm that guy" and hop in the damn car.

■

Getting off a plane and realizing you landed in the wrong city.

602 REASONS TO BE TICKED OFF

Pushy bastards who shove you aside trying to get their luggage off the carousel, as if you only get one crack at it before your bag disappears forever.

 **WHAT TO DO:**

*Yank the bag out of the imperious maggot's
grip and say, "I think you may have grabbed
my bag by mistake. Let's check because I'd hate
for the security guard to have to open fire on
ya over a couple of pairs of underwear." Open
the bag up and start flinging garments back
onto the carousel and say, "Hey, what did you
do with all my stuff?" When he says, "Buddy,
I could have proved it was mine cuz my
name is on the tag," look at the tag and say,
"Listen, you cocky bastard, you're not the only
Maximillion T. Binghampton on the planet."*

602 REASONS TO BE TICKED OFF

Incredibly annoying passengers who think that your head buried in a book means that you want to chat about clouds for six hours.

■

When you tell a lamebrained passenger that you'd prefer to just keep to yourself, and they say they understand because, "People need privacy these days, and you can never get enough time for yourself, and maybe we'll chat later, but how about those Dodgers?"

■

Getting off a plane and realizing you landed in the wrong country.

Cretins trying to ease your mind about flying by comparing it to driving, despite the fact that there is no record of any living person walking around with a neck brace telling people they were "involved in a minor plane crash."

When you're nervous about flying but luckily the flight attendant allays your fears by giving a five-minute talk on not being able to breathe, crashing into the ocean, and getting completely sucked out the doors of the plane.

602 REASONS TO BE TICKED OFF

Putting your back out trying to pry your ass off the suctioning airline toilet seat.

■

When the flight attendant mentions that there are two vital emergency exits on the plane, and you notice that the biggest buffoons you ever laid eyes on are in control of each latch.

MISHAPS

602 REASONS TO BE TICKED OFF

Cooking on a grill and having twelve pounds of meat fall between the racks.

■

Drunken imbeciles who still want a piece of you as the EMTs place you in the back of the ambulance.

■

Falling asleep on the beach and waking up in a burn unit, then overhearing family members pass by your bed and say, "No, that can't be him, let's try the other end of the hall."

Sticking a fork into a cooked egg, and the smoldering yoke explodes and chars your eyeballs.

When you turn a treadmill to a high speed and it sends you careening into the water cooler.

Breaking your foot after angrily kicking a wall because you hurt your arm.

Bench-pressing a ton of weight as you trash-talk the other people in the gym, and then getting stuck under it and having to scream for help.

Bench-pressing no weight at all,
and then getting stuck under the bar
and having to scream for help.

■

Building up your legs on a machine at the
gym as everyone seemingly looks on at your
amazing strength, then the trainer comes
over and informs you that the janitor needs
his industrial cleaning unit back.

■

Looking for a piece of lost eyewear
and then hearing a loud crack.

602 REASONS TO BE TICKED OFF

Spending three hours looking for your eyeglasses and then finally realizing you're wearing them.

■

Thinking you're safe because of the old adage "You can't hit a person with glasses on," then the melee begins and within seconds you have shards of glass in both eyes, you're getting pummeled over the head with crutches, and whipped with the cord of a hearing aid.

■

Losing a testicle climbing over a barbed wire fence.

As you're on the first golf tee with hundreds of people watching, you not only swing and miss, but your club slips out of your hand and lands on the roof of the clubhouse.

 # WHAT TO DO:

Turn so you're facing the clubhouse and yell, "There's that club I said I wanted to return. Give me a merchandise credit and don't ever sell me something like that again." Then walk away muttering, "Two-time course champion and they sell me a defective club."

602 REASONS TO BE TICKED OFF

Squeezing a zit that's not ready and ending up needing a lumpectomy on your face.

■

Driving an automatic transmission after years with a clutch, and out of habit you keep shifting the car into park, while your left foot locks up the brakes of the reeking contraption and sends everyone's head smashing through the windshield.

■

Scraping your dry, cracked lips on a nearly empty cylinder of Chap Stick, so now they're not only dry, they're bleeding.

Walking into a swarm of flies and instead of keeping your mouth shut, you asininely say, "What the hell are these things?" which allows several of them to glide down your throat.

Placing your hide-a-key in a spot you believe nobody will ever look, and two months later *you* can't even remember where you hid the damn thing.

Nearly severing a limb climbing a fence, then realizing the fence ends thirty yards down.

602 REASONS TO BE TICKED OFF

Buying a house that sits "right over the water," but it turns out the water is in your frigging basement.

■

When your house smells like crap because the plumber you hired is an idiot.

■

When you knock out the wrong beam and the ceiling falls on your head, followed by an attic and a roof.

Trying to rip open a large box flap and punching yourself in the face.

■

Burning the hell out of your hands because you picked up something hot, then holding on to it for another excruciating minute because the only place to put it down is on your lap or on top of your grandmother's head.

■

Licking batter off a knife and suddenly wondering why vanilla frosting tastes like blood and has the consistency of tongue.

602 REASONS TO BE TICKED OFF

Brainless family members who see the
ladder up against the side of the house
and you lying face down on the pavement,
and ask "What happened here?"

■

As you see the car in front of you
start to pull out, you turn your head
to the left to wait for an opening, then
you see a tiny one and floor it, only
to find the broken-necked coward
in front of you never went.

Exchanging information after a car accident, then getting in your mangled heap, driving two blocks, and getting in another accident.

Stepping on a patch of ice to see if it's slippery and falling face-first down the side of a mountain.

When your dad, who always says, "You can't cry over spilled milk," beats the piss out of you for spilling your milk.

602 REASONS TO BE TICKED OFF

When your dad hits you so hard with a yard stick, twenty years later you're able to measure stuff with your ass.

■

Catching your mate cheating on you using a position you taught them, only now it's actually generating results.

■

Walking through heavy snow and realizing your brand-new boots fell off two miles ago.

When some idiot thinks your home number is a fax machine and spends an entire month trying to send you a three-thousand-page document.

■

Getting smacked in the head in a crowded room and not knowing who did it.

■

Falling on crutches and breaking your other leg and both arms.

602 REASONS TO BE TICKED OFF

When the vet informs you that the reason your dog keeps mauling you is it's actually a wolf.

■

When your idiotic family wakes up, sees the car parked on the neighbor's lawn and you lying facedown in a pile of vomit, and asks, "Were you out late last night?"

■

Yelling for help and the person who comes to your aid whales the living crap out of you.

When your dad, who always says "You just never know," gives you a whack because "You should have known."

◼

When you buy a new slate pool table and on your first shot you completely miss the cue ball and tear the felt right off the table.

◼

When some inebriated numbskull breaks in pool and airmails the cue ball into your nuts.

602 REASONS TO BE TICKED OFF

Fainting while donating blood, then falling on your skull and ultimately being the one who needs blood.

■

Drunken gluttons suddenly puking all over you with no warning.

■

Hucking a heavy mucus lungi and half of it lands on your chin, while the other half travels all the way to the zenith of your shoe.

Getting your head wedged between
two elevator doors.

■

Playing racquetball for the first time
and running face-first into a transparent
wall as you attempt to enter the court.

■

Shattering your ass bone falling out
an open window you just warned
everyone else to watch out for.

255

602 REASONS TO BE TICKED OFF

Enjoying the view snow skiing and then crashing into a tree.

■

Waiting on the side of a frozen trail for a helicopter to airlift your broken ass to the hospital.

■

Walking to the medical center with ski boots on and falling and breaking some more shit.

Popping a zit on top of your head and having no idea where the pus went.

When the solidly built woman you've been dating mentions something about her "nuts."

Trying to impress people with a fancy card shuffle and spraying half the deck on the floor.

602 REASONS TO BE TICKED OFF

When your chowderheaded family finds you lying in a puddle of blood next to a pile of gambling slips and three of your teeth and asks, "Are you in some kind of trouble?"

■

Overhearing two salesmen laugh about the piece of junk they just sold you.

■

Kicking a ball so hard your shoe flies off and whacks you in the head.

Turning to see what's coming at you
and it wallops you in the face.

■

Trying to split a piece of wood and
the ax bounces off the log, shoots up,
and splits your skull open.

■

Some ignoramus smashing his car
into your house, then his lawyer showing
up and saying it was your fault for
building on that location.

602 REASONS TO BE TICKED OFF

Your hilarious kids tying your shoes together during one of your naps, because what could be funnier than watching a grown man fall face-first into a lit fireplace?

■

Checking someone out across the street as if they'd possibly be interested in you, especially when you're momentarily going to lose five teeth plowing face-first into a lamppost.

Getting a piece of meat lodged in your throat, causing you to thrash about in your chair while the clueless imbeciles at your table remark, "He's had way too much wine."

Choking in a restaurant and your gutless and utterly stupid family members allow some gigantic lummox to wrap you in a bear hug and make choking seem like the the most tremendous feeling in the world.

602 REASONS TO BE TICKED OFF

Anal restaurants that charge you full price for a meal you choked and nearly died on.

◾

When a huge chunk of meat lands on your plate because the lunkhead who was giving the Heimlich didn't have the brains to aim the blue-faced wretch toward people who were done eating.

◾

When the ambulance takes forever to arrive and then runs you over.

When you're in a speeding ambulance
thinking how great it is that cars pull
over so these vehicles can break every
law in the books, then you feel a
tremendous jolt as you slam into
another ambulance.

When you're writhing on the ground
and clutching your bashed skull, and
some dipshit leans in and whispers,
"Tell me what hurts."

602 REASONS TO BE TICKED OFF

Catching a fly ball at a baseball game, and then wishing you hadn't as fifty muscleheads pounce on top of you and start tearing at your flesh like it's cannibal season.

■

Missing with an uppercut that is so poorly thrown it ends up smashing into your own face.

■

Playing tag football with some inane mulyak who thinks "two-hand touch" means it's okay to grab you with both hands and chuck you through the windshield of a parked car.

KIDS, MARRIAGE, AND WEDDINGS

602 REASONS TO BE TICKED OFF

Ending up with a slew of kids because your wife evidently can't count to fourteen on a calendar.

◼

Looking at pictures of your old girlfriend and your wife and wondering if there's a time machine that you could hop into.

◼

Women who can have sixteen kids and actually lose weight during the process, but your pregnant wife grows so large you actually pass the blubberneck in the hall and think, "Who the hell was that broad?"

Doltish parents bringing their kid over to drool on *your* kid's toys, then when they're leaving they casually mention the little maggot has the flu, shingles, and some other virus that has all the doctors scratching their heads.

Ridiculous parents who blame their son's behavior on the fact that he's tired, as if assholes are just people who lack a good night's sleep.

602 REASONS TO BE TICKED OFF

Rude bastards asking if your kid is a boy or a girl, when it's blatantly obvious what it is if you could just tear off the freak's diaper and look.

■

WHAT TO DO:

Tell the ignoramus what the child's gender is and then ask, "How about yourself? Your body says female, but your face says, 'Hold on a second here.'"

Imbecilic diaper companies putting cartoon characters on the front of the diapers that disappear when the kid pees, as if that'll help you train the runt now that he relates pissing his pants with performing magic tricks.

◼

People who say, "Time flies when you have kids," yet you have to seemingly wait forever for your punk kid to grow up so you can boot his ass out of your house.

602 REASONS TO BE TICKED OFF

When you want to scream at your pothead son for smoking drugs but morally can't because you're completely baked and also dealing crack cocaine on the side.

■

Finding drugs in your kid's pockets that are way better than the shit you've been doing, and the little bastard refuses to even tell you where the hell he got it.

When your incredibly naive wife, who constantly complains about having no money, says, "I found a large bag of pure coke in our son's drawer so I flushed it down the toilet."

■

Diving into your septic tank and wading through piles of your family's waste so you can retrieve a bag of coke.

■

Whining, politically correct wretches who say you shouldn't spank your kid's butt with your hand, despite the fact that these are the same demons who flogged their children's backs in the 1960s with leather belts and yardsticks.

602 REASONS TO BE TICKED OFF

The fact that people who say you shouldn't spank kids actually need to be smacked harder than the kids.

■

Using that stupid time-out method on your kid, which basically just gives him a chance to catch his breath before heading out on another mission of pillage and destruction.

■

When your pathetic son threatens to run away from home but every morning you check his bed and the lily-livered poltroon is still there.

When you're at a gathering and people feel compelled to tell you that your kid's diaper needs to be changed, as if it's any business of theirs how you decide to save money.

■

Pulling some immoral scoundrel out of your bed and beating him to a pulp as your wife screams, "This isn't what you think," then realizing she's right because there's at least four more people under the sheets.

602 REASONS TO BE TICKED OFF

When the priest asks the wedding guests if there is any reason why the two dolts shouldn't get married, and no one ever speaks up despite the fact that half of these pairings are an absolute train wreck from the first "I do."

■

When the priest mentions that the newlyweds come from strong families, then you go through the receiving line and meet the groom's old man, his three stepfathers, the biological father, his deadbeat dad, and three women claiming the bride has their DNA.

Sitting at a wedding table with eight vapid dolts who all know each other from college, and they don't seem the slightest bit interested in your ability to drink a Bud with your bare foot.

When your wife strikes up a conversation with the person next to her at a wedding and leaves you staring into the center of a now frigid bun for forty-five minutes.

602 REASONS TO BE TICKED OFF

Sitting at a wedding table pretending to make calls on a cell phone to cover up the fact that you've never been more uncomfortable in your life.

■

Video guys at weddings shoving their instrument of torture in your face for a funny anecdote, as if it's your job to improve the quality of this industriously wretched production that will ultimately be rewound a total of once.

WHAT TO DO:

Make up something that this pinhead will be forced to edit out. "Hi, you phonies. Thanks for ruining my weekend. Beautiful day for golf and I'm watching you fools make utter buffoons out of yourselves on the parquet. Gosh, I hope you got a good deal on this shithole. I found a hair in my soup that must have come off an orangutan. I left it on top of the cake." Then whisper, "Also wanted to let you know that I saw the slime bag who's doing the videoing going through your envelopes. He offered to split it with me, but I said absolutely not! I got him dead to rights so I'm holding out for 60 percent."

602 REASONS TO BE TICKED OFF

Weddings in which the bride is eight months pregnant and all these phonies are yapping about how much in love they are, when it's painfully obvious to anyone with a brain larger than a nipple that this marriage is headed straight to arbitration.

■

Spying the bride and groom at each other's throats after you've already written the check and placed it in the gift pile.

Cheap pricks who rent a friggin' VFW hall for their daughter's wedding that comes complete with a five-minute open bar and a heaping pile of rancid food prepared by some shell-shocked WWII mulyak who had his taste buds sliced off in 1944.

Trying to suck down as many open-bar drinks as you can, but the streetwise function people thwart your plans by placing one agonizingly slow dingbat behind the bar to serve one thousand liver-damaged booze hounds.

602 REASONS TO BE TICKED OFF

When the newlyweds finally make their way to your table to say "Hi" after four agonizing hours making small talk with the plethora of bungholes you're sitting with, and two seconds later the foolish lovestruck pinheads are gone and you don't see them again for half a century.

■

Trying to deliver an eloquent toast for a couple of blowhards who are about to enter into a marriage that is making a beeline for a double homicide.

Stupid cocks giving the toast at a wedding and throwing out that horseshit about "I'm not losing a brother, I'm gaining a sister," when it's numbingly obvious that his brother is lost forever and he's gaining a major pain in the ball sack.

Greedily multiplying $100 times the number of blowhards you invited to your wedding, but ending up with only half the total, in addition to a box of spoons, several bowls, and twenty-two electric mixers.

602 REASONS TO BE TICKED OFF

Miserable cranks trying to bring your marriage down by saying how awful theirs is, as if you linked up with the same heinous bitch they did.

■

When your boozed-up best man gives a moving toast filled with eye-watering anecdotes about you deciding to "finally settle down after wasting all those years wearing your mother's clothes and sleeping with anything that had at least six toes."

Dingbats boasting about how far they traveled to your wedding, as if you'd have given a rat's rectum if the itinerant fools checked off "can't attend" as long as you got your cash.

When your new bride won't agree that the cash is yours and all the forks, knives, and glass shit are hers.

602 REASONS TO BE TICKED OFF

When someone tells you, "Your wife is great," and then walks off leaving you wondering what exactly that means.

■

When a klutz shows up at your wedding giftless and says "I have a year to get you something," when the cheap maggot should say, "I had your two-year engagement to get it and failed, so the chances of me getting it in one are pretty slim."

WHAT TO DO WITH THESE SKINFLINTS:

Tell the imperious frighead, "I also have a year in which to supply you with the chicken dinner you checked off. Give me your name and address so I can have the staff mail out the hormone-riddled carcass as soon as your gift arrives and clears through my account."

602 REASONS TO BE TICKED OFF

Perverted wedding guests who keep tapping their glasses so they can watch a make-out session, instead of sucking down the contents of their glasses and staggering around like a real man scouring for something they can thrust their own tongue into.

■

Women who show up to your wedding in some trampy outfit with their boobs hanging out, as if the lifelong commitment you're about to enter isn't hard enough by itself.

Hiring some sucky band to play at your wedding and when you think they're finally sounding decent, you notice there isn't a soul positioned at any of the instruments.

602 REASONS TO BE TICKED OFF

Wedding bands that flip their lid
when you make a musical request
for them to play more records.

■

Complete ninnies who wink and tell
you on your wedding day, "Tonight you get
to be alone with her," when you've been
living with the wench for a decade and
you both couldn't care less if you ever
saw one another naked again.

Complete buffoons who nearly yank your arm out of its socket as they scream in your ear, "You have to come out and dance to my favorite song!" when you've made it brutally obvious you don't dance by removing your shoes and sneering at anyone who comes near you.

■

☞ WHAT TO DO: ☜

When this leech is done dancing, grab the clown by the arm and drag her over to the bar. Order a shot and pour it into her mouth while screaming, "You have to drink this. It's my favorite liver-corroding poison!" Then drag her over and plop her in a chair next to some old binny. Yell, "You have to talk to her. She's so interesting!" Tap the coot on the shoulder and say, "Please tell her the one about what happened at the bank yesterday. The long version. And take your time cuz she's a little slow!" Then stand off to the side and do some dancing.

602 REASONS TO BE TICKED OFF

Watching the wedding video and seeing evidence of all your "close friends" stealing cash from the gift pile, urinating on your grandmother's shoes, and humping the wedding cake.

■

Overhearing a rumor at the reception that the groom is already cheating, and you can't share the gossip with your wife because she's been AWOL for the last hour and a half.

RIPOFFS

Books written by shameless authors that promise you 602 things, but then you check and there's only 588, counting this one.

AUTHOR'S SOURCES

A-holes, asswipes, boobs, brainless chumps, cluckheads, chowderheads, coleslaw brains, cowards, dimwits, dolts, dunces, feckless morons, goons, half-wits, idiots, inconsiderate louses, klutzes, lummoxes, maggots, neighbors, nimrods, obdurate bastards, old bats, pains in the ass, ridiculous fools, saps, senior shitizens, simpletons, utter dinks, venomous scoundrels, wretches, wussies, and yellow-livered poltroons.